Crossing Anglican Horizons

Crossing Anglican Horizons

A Memoir

SAMUEL VAN CULIN

VTS PRESS
Alexandria, Virginia
2024

VTS PRESS

Virginia Theological Seminary
3737 Seminary Road
Alexandria, VA 22304
www.vts.edu

ISBN: 979-8-3434-3776-8

Typesetting and design by Christopher Poore.

Contents

Acknowledgements

I recognize the importance of three General Conventions of the Episcopal Church—in 1955, 1958, and 1961—where decisions were made that generated new initiatives in the Episcopal Church and brought new dimensions to my vocation as a priest. Likewise, I recognize Lambeth Conference resolutions in 1968 and 1978 which set new directions in inter-Anglican planning and opened new opportunities for me personally.

I am grateful for the leadership and personal support of Presiding Bishops Arthur Lichtenberger, John Hines, and John Allin, and that of many colleagues during my twenty years at the Episcopal Church Center.

It was a special privilege and education to work with two Archbishops of Canterbury—both Archbishops Runcie and Carey—as their leadership role in the Communion expanded and deepened. The Archbishop's convening authority is as critical to the life of the Communion today as it was in their day, and the Secretary General's influence in assisting the Archbishop in "gathering the Communion" is still important.

I am indebted to Philip Chalk—originally an Episcopal Church Volunteer for Mission sent to assist the staff of the ACC in 1985 in developing what become the Anglican Communion Office and now a friend of some forty years—for his continuous and dedicated support in the collection and preservation of these memories and experiences. Philip typed every word through numerous drafts and helped organize and edit the final product.

I am honored and grateful that these modest reflections have been published at the encouragement of the Rev. Dr. Ian Markham, Dean and President of Virginia Theological Seminary, and the Rev. Dr. Katherine Grieb, Director of the Center for Anglican Communion Studies at the Seminary. I would like to include an additional thank you to Dr. Grieb for writing the Foreword. I am grateful to Bishop Anthony Poggo from South Sudan, the current Secretary General of the Anglican Communion, for his thoughtful Afterword. Finally, I am indebted to the Rev. Christopher Poore, editor of VTS Press, for his patient and professional management of the production and publication of this book.

Foreword

THE REV. A. KATHERINE GRIEB

Let me begin by expressing my thanks to the Reverend Canon Samuel Van Culin for his request that I write the foreword to this book which he has modestly subtitled "A Memoir" and which is both that and so much more than that. I have known and admired Sam for many years, and it is a source of personal pride that the first Secretary General of the Anglican Communion (arguably, after the Archbishop of Canterbury, the most important leader of the Anglican Communion) is a graduate of Virginia Theological Seminary and a priest of the Episcopal Church, in addition to everything else he has become and has accomplished.

From the very first pages of this book to its final paragraphs you will hear from a natural leader who, by his considerable talent and dedicated service to the Church, has found himself at the center of some of the most important events in the recent history of the Anglican Communion.

Many of the institutions, organizations, and patterns of Church life that we now take for granted were put in place during Sam's ministry and some of them as a direct result of it: readers may be interested that two historically different congregations became joined as early as 1958 at St. Andrew's Cathedral in Honolulu where Sam was curate of one and rector of the other; other readers will welcome the description of the three General Conventions (1955, 1958, 1961) that resulted in Sam's appointment to the Department of Overseas Mission at the Episcopal Church Center and defined his work; still other readers will welcome information about the Partner Parish program, the Companion Diocese program, and the Anglican Congress of Toronto (1963) that produced "Mutual Responsibility and Interdependence in the Body of Christ" which was prepared by Bishop Stephen Bayne and which led to "Ventures in Mission" in the 1970s and 1980s.

Sam and Terry Waite both worked on hostage release efforts, and they worked together in Uganda on lay training. Sam cooperated with the Port Harcourt project in Nigeria, with Cuttington College in Liberia, with St. Luke's Hospital in Tokyo, and the list goes on and on. He was active in Anglican Consultative Council (ACC) meetings and was Secretary of the Lambeth Conference of 1988, which set up the Eames Commission to deal with the question of the ordination of women to the priesthood and the episcopate, following the ordination of two women as priests in Hong Kong in 1971. Sam worked closely with several Archbishops of Canterbury, talked with Pope John Paul II, and was awarded an honorary O.B.E. by Queen Elizabeth II. That doesn't happen to everyone. It is a privilege to read his thoughtful comments on the way he felt God's leadership in what he calls "a burst of energy for mission."

I believe I am right in saying that originally this book was intended for the considerably smaller audience of Sam's immediate family and close friends, but when I heard about it, I entreated him to rethink that decision and to expand his reflections to include much more information about the events of his vocation, which I am confident will interest a much greater audience than he had anticipated. I continue to believe that what may look like a small book will turn out to be of major importance to anyone interested in the recent history of the Anglican Communion and in the deep desire of its leaders to witness to and support God's mission to the world. Sam is reflecting theologically on his considerable experience as he recounts the events and discussions about them that have shaped much of our contemporary discourse about mission.

A few examples of these theological reflections will have to suffice in this short space. Sam cites Reinhold Niebuhr's *Moral Man and Immoral Society* (1932): "A rational ethic aims at justice, and a religious ethic makes love the ideal," a idea that also influenced the Reverend Dr. Martin Luther King, Jr. and, more recently, Nicholas Wolterstorff. The Niebuhrs and Paul Tillich, the Clinical Pastoral Education movement, and the work of psychotherapist Carl Jung have remained important to Sam throughout his ministry.

The theology of Bishop Stephen Bayne, the Executive Secretary of the Anglican Communion under Archbishop of Canterbury Geoffrey Fisher, as summarized in the title of the key 1963 report "Mutual Responsibility and Interdependence in the Body of Christ" has clearly shaped Sam's thinking. So has the theology of Robert Runcie, Archbishop of Canterbury from 1980 to 1991. Asked to describe the task of the Archbishop of Canterbury, Runcie replied, "The job of the Archbishop of Canterbury is to gather the Communion, not to rule it." Sam appreciated the "convening" and "mobilizing" aspect of his leadership and described his own work as assisting that strategy. He also appreciated Runcie's addition to his Invitation to Lambeth Conference 1988: "I want each bishop to bring their diocese with them" and the Archbishop's response to Pope John Paul II's warning that "a sympathetic consideration of women's ordination would introduce an additional 'impediment' to Anglican-Roman Catholic relationships." Runcie replied that the theological warrant for proceeding was the Anglican conviction that "the priesthood of Christ offers the whole of humanity back to the Father," which an exclusively male priesthood could not do. Sam chooses to end his book with a reference to Runcie's words, "At the heart of our faith is a cross, and not, as in some religions, an eternal calm." One of the reasons I love this book is that its author is attentive to the theological ideas that have guided the implementation of God's mission as he saw it.

Another one of the reasons I am grateful for the opportunity to commend this book to you is that Samuel Van Culin and I share deep commitments to a number of people and the places they inhabit, places like Lambeth Palace and the Anglican Communion Office in London, where Sam served for twelve years as Secretary General, first of the Anglican Consultative Council, then of the entire Anglican Communion; The Cathedral Church of Christ at Canterbury, where Sam was a canon and is now Canon Emeritus; The Washington National Cathedral of Saints Peter and Paul, where Sam has been a canon more recently; St. John's Church, Lafayette Square, from which the Friends of Canterbury Cathedral in the United States (FOCCUS) originated, on whose board we both serve; The Episcopal Church Center, 815 Second Avenue, NYC, where Sam worked for and then headed the Department of Overseas Missions, and whose Global Partnerships and Mission Office continues to do wonderful work; St. Thomas Church, Fifth Avenue, NYC, where Sam preached and presided at the Eucharist during his twenty-one years in New York City, which no doubt fed the musical part of his soul; and, of course, Virginia Theological Seminary, which has played a very important role in both of our lives.

Enjoy this book and meet or reconnect with a wonderful man who has done a lot of good in the name of Jesus Christ and seems to have thoroughly relished doing it.

The Rev. A. Katherine Grieb, J.D., Ph.D., L.L.M.
Priest, Diocese of Washington in the Episcopal Church
Director of the Center for Anglican Communion Studies
Virginia Theological Seminary

Crossing Anglican Horizons

SAMUEL VAN CULIN

Beginning

One of the advantages of old age is that I have had the opportunity to reflect on the experiences and events of my life. Now in my ninety-forth year, I have been asked to share a selection of memories that I find meaningful, which may help in an appreciation of the way the Episcopal Church and the wider Anglican Communion became more involved in the global mission of the church after the Second World War. What is recorded here are bits of memory in old age.

I remember vividly, as a boy, standing at Waikiki Beach and Ala Moana in Honolulu, looking out to sea and wondering, "What is beyond the horizon?" The bombing of Pearl Harbor in 1941 led me to my first journey beyond that horizon, and my life at Princeton University (1948–52) led me further. But it was joining the priesthood of the Episcopal Church and the Anglican Communion that opened the biggest world to me—beyond and above the horizons of my childhood. Let me explain.

A Wartime Youth

I was born on Sept. 20, 1930, at Queen's Hospital in Honolulu, Hawaii. My mother was Susie Ellen Mossman, a fourth-generation Hawaiian islander. As a boy, I was told that my mother's great-great-grandparents, Captain Thomas and Maryann Mossman, arrived in Hawaii from Britain with their four children in 1849. Their son and my maternal great-grandfather, Thomas Mossman, was married to Akula Hooneiaina—the cousin, according to family tradition, of Hawaii's Queen Emma. Thomas and Akula's son, Ralph Mossman, married Rebecca Mellish, my grandmother. My mother Susie, the daughter of Ralph and Rebecca, was one of eight children. I grew up with numerous aunts, uncles, and cousins—very much the Hawaiian way.

On my father's side, I am descended from Huguenots who left Le Puy, France in the late 1600s and settled in Goochland County, Virginia. Part of that family later moved to Philadelphia, and many of them were buried in the Woodlands Cemetery there in the 1800s. My father, for whom I was named, was born in January 1901 and came to Hawaii following the end of WWI, in which he served in the US Navy. Embracing and integrating the varied elements of Hawaiian, French, Scottish, and English culture inherited from my parents has been an engaging interest throughout my life. My brother, Thomas Myers Van Culin, was born eight years after me and named for our paternal grandmother's family.

I was educated at the Punahou School, founded in Honolulu in 1841 by early New England missionaries who introduced Christianity to the Kingdom of Hawaii. The multicultural background of my classmates and the experiences we shared in the "Hawaiian environment" were important in helping me understand myself and the world I was growing up in.

My early education was interrupted by the Japanese attack on Pearl Harbor on December 7, 1941. I was eleven years old at the time, and I have carried the memory of that event throughout my life. I was too young then to realize the tremendous impact of the Pearl Harbor attack on my personal life and on the life of my country. While the attack caused a disruption for me, I came eventually to realize that by bringing the United States into World War II, it inaugurated an historic change in the global relationships of my country. These recalibrated global relationships have influenced the rest of my life.

Following the attack, my mother, serving in the Honolulu Health Department, helped to provide emergency health services to the injured from Pearl Harbor, Hickam Airfield, and other affected military establishments. She was providing an essential service and hence was not free to help the family deal with the displacements caused by the attack.

As a result, in early 1942, my brother and I were sent to live with a family in California's San Joaquin Valley. I was about eleven years old and my brother was three when we sailed from Honolulu to San Diego on the British ship Aquitania, accompanied by naval escort vessels because of reports of German submarines in the Pacific. Dos Palos, where we settled, was a small town in the central San Joaquin Valley, a farming community where, as part of the student-volunteer war service, I learned how to pick cotton, tomatoes, and garlic on farms that had been seized from Japanese-Americans after their forced relocation to internment camps. Additionally, I planted my first Victory Garden, raised chickens and rabbits, and attended Dos Palos Joint Union School. I grew to realize that this was an "early immigrant experience" in my life, exposing me to a different world from that in which I was born and would live.

My brother and I returned to Honolulu and the Punahou School in 1943, when fear of another Japanese attack on Hawaii had passed. I had to readjust to Hawaiian life after leaving the starkly different world of Dos Palos. Initially,

Punahou classes were held at the Teachers College at the University of Hawaii because the school's campus had been taken over for the war effort; students would return to the campus only at the end of the war. In addition to my studies, I participated in theatrical productions and was elected president of the student body my senior year. Also, during that year, I composed "The Ballad of Punahou," a choral work performed by my classmates at our graduation ceremony in June of 1948.

Van Culin with his father and mother upon his departure from Honolulu for Princeton University, 1948.

College and Seminary

As for college, my original preference had been Bowdoin College in Brunswick, Maine, but John Fox, the Punahou School president, urged me to apply to Princeton University. He eventually convinced me. I started at Princeton in September 1948 and was fortunate to obtain two scholarships, which enabled me to spend the full four years there. Without them, I could not have afforded it. I majored in medieval and modern European history with a minor in religion. Under the influence of history professors T.E. Mommsen, E.H. Harbison, W.P. "Buzzer" Hall, G.A. Craig, and J.R. Strayer, as well as religion professor R.P. Ramsey, I grew to appreciate the centuries of development of Western civilization and the role of the Christian church and culture in its gradual formation. As stimulating as this course of study was, I grew to realize its limitation. There was no coursework in Asian, African, or Middle Eastern studies; this has been corrected in the current Princeton curriculum, and women, of course, also have been added to the student body since my day.

I sang in the Princeton Chapel Choir, under the leadership of Carl Weinrich. This experience introduced me over a period of three years to the rich treasures of church music—particularly to the works of Lassus, Monteverde, and de Victoria. Music had always been an important part of my life, beginning with Hawaiian music during my childhood. The Princeton Chapel Choir experience expanded that interest and pleasure, as did my involvement in the Triangle Club, which produced an annual musical variety show written and produced by students. (Triangle alumni include such well-known figures as Jose Ferrar and Jimmy Stewart; the group was also a favorite of F. Scott Fitzgerald's during his Princeton years.) As president of the Triangle Show in 1951–52, I was invited to join members of the cast as a guest on both the Ed Sullivan TV Show and The Stork Club television show, hosted by Sherman Billingsly. Through Triangle, I developed a love of the history of Broadway theater and music, and my years at Princeton helped me to appreciate music's magnificent cultural diversity.

In my last year at Princeton, I struggled to decide whether to go to law school or seminary. Law seemed the appropriate step into a life of political and public service, which had always attracted me. But Princeton had opened the world of European Christian culture and development, so I decided to go to seminary, convinced that I would be a better lawyer eventually if I had a theological education.

Graduating from Princeton in 1952, I enrolled in Virginia Theological Seminary (VTS) in Alexandria, Virginia, as a candidate for ordination from the Episcopal Diocese of Hawaii. At VTS, I was drawn into a theological awakening, studying the works of Reinhold and H. Richard Niebuhr, and Paul Tillich. Under the influence of professors Albert Mollegen and Clifford Stanley, I acquired a deeper appreciation of the prophetic vocation of the church— remembering especially the Niebuhrian comment, "A rational ethic aims at justice, and a religious ethic makes love the ideal." It was in reading Tillich that I first realized the natural affinity and partnership between theology and psychology in their exploration of human nature and culture. In turn, this led me to a deeper appreciation of the church's pastoral vocation.

An important element in the curriculum at VTS was the program of "Clinical Pastoral Psychology," organized by Dr. Ruel Howe. The program required a summer's experience in a therapeutic setting, which I satisfied at Connecticut's Norwich State Hospital, working with patients and observing treatment. It was this clinical study and experience that introduced me to the work of two major late-nineteenth- and early-twentieth-century psychotherapists, Sigmund Freud of Vienna and Carl Jung of Zurich, and I came away with what would be a continuing interest in the life and work of Jung. As a result, any interest in pursuing a law degree faded away.

St. Andrew's Cathedral in Honolulu, Hawaii, where Van Culin was baptized, confirmed, and ordained. He served here as his first post following his graduation from seminary in 1955. Courtesy the Episcopal Diocese of Hawai'i.

A Young Priest

I was ordained to the priesthood in the Episcopal Church on St. Andrew's Day, 1955, at St. Andrew's Cathedral, Honolulu.

The cathedral was commissioned in 1862 by King Kamehameha IV and Queen Emma. King Kamehameha IV produced the first prayer book in Hawaiian, translating the Book of Common Prayer from the Church of England. During my later service as Secretary General of the Anglican Communion, I was invited by the librarian at the Lambeth Palace Library to see a book he thought I might find interesting. Indeed, I did: it was a printed copy of the Hawaiian prayer book, and on the inside front cover Kamehameha IV had written in his own hand an inscription to the Lord Bishop of London, granting him, with respect, ownership of that copy of the prayer book.

At the time of my ordination, there were two separate congregations worshipping in the cathedral, one

Hawaiian—composed of people from Asian and Hawaiian backgrounds—and one haole (a Hawaiian term for people who are not native to Hawaii and who usually are of white, Anglo-Saxon background). I served for two years as a curate in the haole congregation before becoming the rector of the Hawaiian congregation; in 1958, the two congregations were joined as a result. St. Andrew's Cathedral was then home to a worshipping community that included Caucasian, Hawaiian, Filipino, Japanese, Chinese, and mixed ethnicities.

In 1958, I was invited to take a curacy post at St. John's Episcopal Church in Washington, D.C.—"The Church of the Presidents" directly across Lafayette Square from the White House. During those years at St. John's, I introduced the parish to the Seabury Series, a new Christian education curriculum from the national Episcopal Church that drew on insights from contemporary psychology and offered components aimed at children, youth, and adults. This further convinced me of the vital partnership between theology and psychology.

During the 1950s, the Episcopal Church, along with American society as a whole, was responding to its new global relationships and responsibilities following World War II. Through such programs and agencies as the Marshall Plan and the United States Agency for International Development (USAID), large numbers of Americans were going abroad to live and work. At the same time, the Episcopal Church was becoming newly familiar with parts of the Anglican Communion in Africa, the Middle East, Latin America, and Asia—regions which had been evangelized by British and Australian missionary agencies that now were turning to us for joint missionary initiatives.

While in Washington, I became involved in the Overseas Mission Society, known commonly by the acronym OMS and organized by a group of local laity and clergy. Through OMS, I helped launch Layman International (LI), a training initiative for Americans working overseas that provided orientations to the religious traditions and communities in the international locales where participants would be serving. These orientation sessions were administered in cooperation with such organizations as the then-new USAID. My association with St. John's Church, Lafayette Square, as well as with the OMS and LI provided a unique opportunity to be part of a community of concerned Christians exploring the interaction of faith and culture in a new, global perspective.

An Awakening

What we were doing in Washington was typical of the Episcopal Church at large, as I had first observed at the church's 1955 General Convention in Honolulu, which I had attended fresh from seminary. One of the resolutions adopted at that convention had called for the Department of Overseas Mission at the Church Center (the church headquarters in New York City) to organize similar departments of overseas mission at the diocesan level, so as "to foster continuity, knowledge, and support of overseas missionary work" in each diocese. By the General Convention of 1958, this interest had grown significantly, and a resolution was adopted to appoint a committee to help the church grow into "greater understanding, support, and service in its worldwide mission." This committee was chaired by Bishop Walter Gray of Connecticut and was known commonly as the Gray Commission.

At the next General Convention in 1961, the Gray

Commission presented its recommendations in "The Report of the Committee on Overseas Mission"—a comprehensive and specific outline of programs through which every member of the Episcopal Church would be invited to engage in a new commitment to the global mission of the church. The Department of Overseas Mission (also known as the Overseas Department) at the Church Center in New York City decided to appoint an officer with responsibility for implementing the resolutions of the 1961 General Convention, which drew from recommendations by the Gray Commission. I was invited by Presiding Bishop Arthur Lichtenberger to move to New York and assume this new position.

In accepting this post, I would be taking on a responsibility that had been called for by three different General Conventions—1955, 1958, and 1961—and that had been recognized as important to the global commitments of the Episcopal Church. What I did not realize at the time was that I was beginning a ministry in the worldwide Anglican Communion.

Church Center, New York

I arrived in New York City in 1961, beginning what would be twenty-one years of ministry at the Episcopal Church's international headquarters under three Presiding Bishops—Arthur Lichtenberger, John Hines, and John Allin. In my appointment to the Overseas Department, my chief responsibility was to assist the Episcopal Church in developing a more conscious awareness of, and participation in, worldwide mission. My efforts were instrumental in the launch of several programs aimed at fulfilling the goals of the Gray Report, including the Partner Parish program; the Companion Diocese program; and the Program of Special Projects, a fundraising office through which US congregations and dioceses opened new sets of relationships with Anglican counterparts overseas.

In August 1963, I served on the administrative staff of an "Anglican Congress" in Toronto at which episcopal, clerical, and lay representatives from across the international Anglican Communion gathered to reflect on the Communion's global ministry. The reports that were presented and discussed at the Congress were the result of four years of research and consultation and were prepared by the Rt. Rev. Stephen Bayne, a former Bishop of Olympia who was serving as Executive Secretary of the Anglican Communion, having been appointed by the Archbishop of Canterbury, Geoffrey Fisher.

The principal result of the Congress was a final statement of "Mutual Responsibility and Interdependence in the Body of Christ," which came to be known simply as MRI. This document proved to be the critical roadmap in the years that followed the Congress, as the Anglican Communion began to replace centralized structures and habits with global, cooperative forms.

Within months—at its 1964 General Convention in St. Louis—the Episcopal Church acted on MRI by launching "Projects for Partnership," a sweeping effort to conduct international mission activity in closer cooperation with mission agencies from a number of other Anglican provinces and with local Anglican dioceses themselves. Notably, mission programs undertaken through Projects for Partnership were prioritized by the bishops in the diocese where the programs were to operate, opening new lines of communication in the global Communion and incorporating planning in the mission field itself.

A Burst of Energy
for Mission

The MRI report and the initiatives it inspired created the theological and institutional opportunities that would define the rest of my working life. In my post in the Overseas Department, I served as a coordinator of national-level Projects for Partnership activity, beginning with a first wave of proposals in 1965 that included no fewer than 250 projects around the world. In the years that followed, I would represent the Episcopal Church in collaborative discussions among missionary societies based in the US, England, Canada, New Zealand, and Australia while overseeing mission work on the part of the Episcopal Church in Africa, the Middle East, Latin America, and Asia. In this latter role, I supervised personnel, negotiated budgets, inaugurated mission projects, and befriended local church and community leaders.

The Projects for Partnership effort would culminate in the 1970s and early 80s in "Ventures in Mission," a mission-focused fundraising campaign launched by Presiding

*The Very Rev. John Murray Allin, who launched
the Ventures in Mission fundraising campaign.*

Bishop Allin that eventually raised $170 million to fund
mission work in the US and abroad. One of many enduring
legacies of Projects for Partnership is the large number of
companion-diocese and companion-parish links between
local churches in the US and those overseas.

As I look back on these years, I realize that we in the Overseas Department concentrated often on training and development projects. We made missionary appointments to St. Andrew's Seminary in Manila, to the Anglican Seminary in Singapore, and to theological education in Tanzania. In the Middle East, we also made appointments to St. George's College in Jerusalem and ecumenical training initiatives in Beirut.

We also developed a particular focus on missionary partnerships in Africa. The Anglican churches in Africa were developed largely by Anglican missionary societies from England, Australia, and New Zealand. The single exception was Liberia, which was a missionary diocese of the Episcopal Church. Following World War II, the Anglican provinces of East Africa, West Africa, Central Africa, and South Africa were established as independent Anglican provinces and turned to the US to expand their missionary partnerships.

In Uganda, we helped to expand the work of Bishop Tucker Theological College and of Makerere University through missionary appointments and financial grants. Also, a request came from the church to assist in developing a lay training and leadership program for the dioceses of the church in Uganda. I was able to engage the services of Terry Waite to develop this program. Terry was serving with the Church Army in England at the time and moved his family to Uganda to undertake this new responsibility. (A number of years later, Terry joined Archbishop Runcie's staff at

Lambeth Palace, where he became involved in hostage-release efforts in Iran and Lebanon undertaken by both the British and US governments. Terry himself became a hostage eventually in Beirut.)

In the Anglican Church in Nigeria, we cooperated in the development of the Port Harcourt Project, located at the center of Nigerian oil production. This effort was established to minister to new and fast-growing communities caught up in the new petroleum developments. We focused on the local parish church and its school and on the development of the Missions to Seamen. In the Province of Central Africa, we helped with the establishment of a provincial secretary office to coordinate mission planning in the dioceses of Malawi, Zambia, Mashonaland, and Matabeleland. All of our mission initiatives were part of a cooperative enterprise involving companion dioceses, Projects for Partnership, seminary mission societies, the United Thank Offering, Trinity Parish Wall Street's projects office, and Anglican missionary societies in England, Wales, Scotland, Canada, Australia, New Zealand, and others.

Other projects launched in the Overseas Department included the expansion of Cuttington College in Liberia, in cooperation with the Universities and Hospitals Program of the US State Department. In Tokyo, Japan, we participated in the relocation of St. Luke's International Hospital, with the cooperation of key staff from St. Luke's Episcopal Hospital in New York City.

On August 2, 1976, I was appointed Executive for National and World Mission by Presiding Bishop John Allin. As a press release from the Episcopal News Service reported,

> In his new position Mr. Van Culin will work directly with both overseas and U.S. dioceses of the Episcopal Church and with member churches in the Anglican Communion, coordinating and administering a wide variety of programs and relationships which link the national Church with its 113 jurisdictions and other churches around the world.

Life in the Big Apple

During the twenty-one years that I spent in New York City at the Episcopal Church Center, I was an associate priest at St. Thomas Episcopal Church on Fifth Avenue. Though I travelled extensively around the world in those years in fulfillment of my responsibilities, I am grateful that I was a continuing part of the sacramental and liturgical life of St. Thomas's when I was at home in New York City.

I also was involved in the establishment of the C.G. Jung Foundation in New York City. I was a member of the foundation board from 1967 to 1976 and president of the board from 1971 to 1976. During this period, a property was purchased on East 39th Street in Manhattan between Madison and Park Avenues, and the C.G. Jung Center was established. Today, it has a training center for analysts, a library, an archival collection, and an ongoing program of public lectures and education. It is one of a growing number of Jung Centers in the US and around the world. During that time, I undertook psychoanalysis with Dr. M. Esther Harding, a British-American who was the first significant Jungian psychoanalyst in the United States. At her death, she left her estate for the funding of the C.G. Jung Center in New York City.

Jungian analyst Dr. M. Esther Harding, whose estate made possible the founding of the C.G. Jung Center in Manhattan.

London and the Anglican Consultative Council

From New York, I moved to London in 1983 to serve as the Secretary General of the Anglican Consultative Council, or ACC. In a farewell note to me, Presiding Bishop John Allin wrote,

> I share a great consensus that you are needed as Secretary General of the ACC and rejoice in your appointment. At the same time, you will be greatly missed in the Church Center of ECUSA.

My appointment was announced by *The New York Times* in the October 31, 1982 edition:

> As secretary general of the Anglican Consultative Council, which has its headquarters in London, Father Van Culin will be responsible for coordinating the activities of the 28 provinces of the Anglican Communion . . .
>
> In announcing the appointment in London, Archbishop [of Canterbury Robert] Runcie said of Fr. Van Culin: "He is someone who already seems to belong to

the whole Anglican Communion, rather than to any one province. He is known and respected all over the world for the warmth of his friendship and range of his abilities."

Before I left New York, my parish, St. Thomas's Church on Fifth Avenue, held a "commissioning ceremony," at which the Presiding Bishop celebrated and at which I was sent on to my new post in London with prayer. Also, before my departure, the Bishop of New York, Paul Moore, invited me to the Plaza Hotel to address a dinner of the Church Club of New York, a group of clergy and leading lay persons of the diocese. It provided me with the opportunity to describe the ACC.

Including both clergy and laity, the Anglican Consultative Council had been established in the 1960s to provide the Anglican Communion with a broad, consultative body in an effort to implement the mission initiatives called for in the MRI report from the Anglican Congress in Toronto. Its constitution was drafted at a meeting in Kandy, Sri Lanka, in June of 1967 by a committee of which I was a member. The draft constitution was submitted as Resolution 69 to the Lambeth Conference 1968, where it was approved. It was then submitted to all the provinces of the Anglican Communion for review and approval. More than two-thirds of the provinces approved, and the council held its first meeting in Limuru, Kenya, in 1971. At that meeting, the council appointed Bishop John Howe of the

Members of the committee drafting the constitution for the Anglican Consultative Council visiting the Temple of the Tooth in the city of Kandy, Ceylon (now Sri Lanka), June 1967. From left, Mrs. Walker Taylor, wife of the photographer; The Rt. Rev. Ralph Dean, Executive Secretary of the Anglican Communion; The Most Rev. Lakdasa De Mel, Archbishop of Calcutta and Metropolitan of India, Burma, Pakistan, and Ceylon; The Rev. Canon Sam Van Culin; The Rt. Rev. Lakshman Wickremasinghe, Bishop of Kurunegala, Ceylon; The Rev. David Peyton, Church of England; The Warden and Keeper of the Temple of the Tooth; The Rev. Ernie Jackson, Assistant Secretary of the Anglican Communion; and The Most Rev. Leonard Beecher, Archbishop of the Province of East Africa.

Scottish Episcopal Church as its first secretary general. I succeeded him in January 1983.

Soon after my arrival in London, I was welcomed at a reception at Lambeth Palace, at which the Archbishop announced, "We have found our new Secretary General from the Hawaiian Islands." I was pleased that my Hawaiian roots were recognized as part of my vocation and priesthood. Following the reception, Archbishop and Mrs. Runcie hosted a dinner including Presiding Bishop Allin and Mrs. Allin. After dinner, as we gathered informally, I played the piano and sang one of my favorite Gershwin songs, "You've Got That Thing." That prompted the Presiding Bishop to join me at the piano to reprise one of our duets from our traveling days together—one of his favorite songs, "I Met a Million-Dollar Baby at a Five-and-Ten-Cent Store." After some encouragement, Archbishop Runcie, accompanied by Mrs. Runcie, sang a favorite of his, "Joshua, Joshua, Sweeter Than Lemon Squash You Are." I realized that evening how grateful I was for these two mentors and friends.

Van Culin with Archbishop of Canterbury Robert Runcie
visiting the University of the South in Sewanee, Tennessee,
in the mid-1980s.

Secretary General of the Anglican Communion

An early meeting in 1983 with Archbishop Runcie after my arrival in London provided the opportunity to discuss the place of the ACC in Anglican polity. The Archbishop explained that there had been some tension at the Lambeth Conference of 1978 over the appropriate role of the ACC within the Communion. Many bishops, he told me, wanted the assurance that the ACC would not be considered a replacement, as had been suggested, for either of the other two established "symbols of unity" among Anglicans—the Lambeth Conference of Bishops or the Meeting of Primates (the latter being a regular gathering of the heads of each self-governing Anglican province). This tension at the 1978 Lambeth Conference, he added, had affected the gathered bishops' discussions and effectiveness, and this was acknowledged, however obliquely, in Resolution 12 of the 1978 conference:

The Conference asks the Archbishop of Canterbury, as

31

President of the Lambeth Conference and President of the Anglican Consultative Council, with all the primates of the Anglican Communion, within one year to initiate consideration of the way to relate together the international conferences, councils, and meetings within the Anglican Communion so that the Anglican Communion may best serve God within the context of the one, holy, catholic, and apostolic church.

The Archbishop instructed me to assist him in implementing the 1978 Lambeth Conference Resolution 12. It was essential, he said, that these relationships not drift into any kind of "power struggle," but that they be managed carefully and thoughtfully in the spirit of mutuality. He made clear that as the new Secretary General, I now would be expected not only to assist in coordinating the life and work of the ACC, but also to coordinate the Meeting of Primates and the Lambeth Conference itself. Henceforth, I functioned as Secretary General of the Anglican Communion, and all of my successors have been designated with this title. It was thus an office inaugurated by Archbishop Runcie, as a result of the Lambeth Conference resolution and with the support of the officers of the ACC. This resulted in the need to reorganize the ACC staff into an "Anglican Secretariat" staff (now called the Anglican Communion office). Fortunately, this was done with a sense of cooperation and commitment from my colleagues, for which I was grateful. We designed our new stationery to show that we were the "Anglican Secretariat, serving the

Van Culin with Archbishop of Canterbury Robert Runcie at a meeting in Wales.

Archbishop of Canterbury, The Lambeth Conference, the Primates Meeting, and the Anglican Consultative Council." The Secretariat staff continues to this day to be distinguished in its knowledge and creative engagement with the missionary and ecumenical imperatives of the Anglican Communion.

In thinking of the nature of this office, I recalled an occasion in which Archbishop Runcie was asked, "What would you say is the job of the Archbishop of Canterbury?"

He replied, "The job of the Archbishop of Canterbury is to gather the Communion, not to rule it."

This was a powerful image for me, suggesting that leadership has a "convening" and "mobilizing" quality to it, rather than a directing and ordering motivation. It follows that the job of the Anglican Secretariat is one of assisting and supporting the Archbishop in the "gathering" of the Communion.

Getting to Work

From its first meeting in Limuru, Kenya, in 1971, the Anglican Consultative Council has emerged as the major body planning for the Anglican Communion between Lambeth Conferences. Early on, I began to realize that its "consultative" nature was its most valuable asset. The Primates Meetings and the Lambeth Conferences became more focused on questions of authority while the ACC is more focused on questions of mission. Its first meeting in Kenya highlighted partnership in the Anglican Communion (ACC-1, Res. 5). At its second meeting in Dublin, the ACC explored missionary planning, implementation, and support (ACC-2, Res. 59). A survey of subsequent ACC reports over the years demonstrates a focus on the broad outlines of an "arch of mission." It was my responsibility to reinforce the mission orientation of the ACC.

By the time of the ACC's seventh meeting in Singapore in 1987, a report from the "Mission Issues and Strategy

Group" (MIASG) was received. This report became the basis for staff work in developing cooperative planning and action between all missionary societies, agencies, provinces, dioceses, and councils of the Communion, and also with numerous ecumenical agencies. To achieve this, it was necessary to aggregate a host of grassroots initiatives into a series of selective networks—for example, the Communication Network, the Family Network, the Liturgical Network, the Anglican Women Network, and the Ecumenical Network. We inaugurated the office of Anglican Communion Representative at the United Nations in New York City with the appointment of Paul Reeves as our first representative. He had served as the Anglican Archbishop of New Zealand and also as the Governor-General of New Zealand. He developed our UN office with dramatic effectiveness.

Soon after taking office, I organized a meeting of the primates, also in Limuru, in late 1983. At that meeting, among other considerations, the Archbishop asked the primates for their advice as to whether there should be another Lambeth conference and, if one should be held, what concerns it might address. With their support, consultation and preparation began in earnest for a Lambeth Conference of Bishops in Canterbury in 1988.

An Agenda Takes Shape

Subsequently, the sixth and seventh meetings of the Anglican Consultative Council—in Nigeria and Singapore respectively—devoted time to discussing possible themes for the coming Lambeth Conference. The Archbishop and I also began developing a prospective conference agenda designed to satisfy the reservations of bishops frustrated with their experience at the Lambeth Conference in 1978. I became aware of this frustration during an early meeting with the bishops of the church in New Zealand. They reported that in 1978 they had experienced a sense of disappointment, feeling that they had very little of value that they could bring back to their dioceses from the conference. At a meeting on Waihiki Island, we discussed the hope that if they came to Lambeth 1988, they would engage in issues that were germane to the church in New Zealand

I reported this conversation to Archbishop Runcie on

Van Culin escorts Diana, Princess of Wales, at the Queen's Garden Party at Buckingham Palace, held for bishops attending the 1988 Lambeth Conference.

my return and, as a result, in announcing later that he was calling a Lambeth Conference for the summer of 1988, the Archbishop added, "I want each bishop to bring their diocese with them." To satisfy this request from the Archbishop, a series of regional meetings was held around the Communion in Africa, Asia, the Americas, and the Middle East. The meetings included a program of preparatory studies developed to help bishops "bring their diocese with them." Meanwhile, the ACC established working networks in every province to share information about and provide support for programs addressing family relationships, peace and justice issues, the AIDS crisis, interfaith relationships, ecumenical relationships, the environment, and pastoral and dogmatic matters.

Time for prayer and Bible study was a priority. The Bishop of Winchester, John V. Taylor, produced a study of the scriptures entitled "Briefing the Apostles," which provided material for discussion at the daily Bible study. In thinking about how to use this material, I became aware of a very creative experience of Bible study at the Vatican during an assembly of Roman Catholic bishops convened by Pope John Paul II in late 1985 to review the achievements of Vatican II. I wanted to know more about this experience at the Vatican, realizing that this could help us plan our own Bible study groups more creatively. I was informed that Cardinal Godfried Danneels, Archbishop of Mechelen-Brussels, had been the rapporteur, or secretary, of the Vatican assembly. I contacted Cardinal Danneels, suggesting that I visit him, and he welcomed the suggestion. During our conversation in Brussels, he said that the key to the success of their Bible study groups was the fact that each group was composed of members who spoke different languages. As a result, we decided to incorporate that diversity in our Bible studies. This required complex arrangements for translation.

As an example, in a group with English- and Japanese-speaking bishops, translations from English to Japanese and back required a special attentiveness. Bishops began speaking of their daily Bible study very enthusiastically, referring to the unusual experience of considering scripture in an unfamiliar language. We had to handle translation in Portuguese, Japanese, Swahili, Spanish, and English. It proved to be an important experience and a lesson of the impact of culture on biblical interpretation.

One of the interesting dimensions in planning the Lambeth Conference was the task of organizing, with Buckingham Palace, the garden party given by Queen Elizabeth at the palace for the bishops and their spouses. As part of the preparation, I was invited to a small luncheon at Buckingham Palace, hosted by the Queen and Prince Philip. It provided a memorable opportunity for private conversation.

I was one of six luncheon guests. On arrival at the palace, I was met by an equerry and escorted to a pre-luncheon gathering for sherry and conversation. I was greeted by Prince Philip, who spoke of his interest in a special endangered Hawaiian goose, the nene. I expressed gratitude for his work with the World Wildlife Fund to protect and restore the nene in its Hawaiian habitat. I had seen a group of nene at the Slimbridge Wetland Centre in Gloucestershire, where they were breeding them for preparation for their resettlement in Hawaii.

Following lunch, I was invited by an equerry to accompany the Queen so that we could have an opportunity to speak. We discussed recent political unrest in Polynesia, as well as the dog-breeding efforts that she and her sister had undertaken, which, she told me, had produced a Dachshund-Corgi mix that she and Princess Margaret referred to as a "Dorgi." I found her relaxed and easy in conversation, with a mixture of insight and humor.

The Lambeth Conference, 1988

The twelfth Lambeth Conference convened at the University of Canterbury in the summer of 1988. It was the largest ever held to date—518 bishops, compared with seventy-six in 1867. It was recognized from the outset that the subject of the ordination of women to the priesthood and episcopate—a pressing issue for a number of churches—was potentially the most contentious and critical subject on the agenda. The issue of the ordination of women had arisen in China in 1944, when the Bishop of Hong Kong, R.O. Hall, ordained Florence Li Tim-Oi, a female deacon, to the priesthood to meet pastoral and sacramental needs in portions of his diocese isolated by three-sided warfare on the mainland. The "irregularity" of the Hong Kong ordination had led to widespread discussion in the churches of the Communion. In 1971, the Anglican Consultative Council expressed "goodwill toward ordaining women deacons to the priesthood." Soon, Bishop Gilbert Baker of Hong

Kong ordained two women to the priesthood, and a number of additional ordinations of women would follow in the US, Canada, New Zealand, Kenya, and Uganda during the next twelve years. Therefore, the Lambeth Conference of 1988 gave the subject of female ordination prominence on its agenda.

Related controversy was intensified by a communication from Pope John Paul II to Archbishop of Canterbury Runcie prior to the conference, indicating that a sympathetic consideration of women's ordination would introduce an additional "impediment" to Anglican-Roman Catholic relationships. In responding to the Pope, Archbishop Runcie confirmed that the theological foundation for ordaining women was based on the conviction in the Anglican Church that "the priesthood of Christ offers the whole of humanity back to the Father." Therefore, a priesthood that is exclusively male is not fully adequate, in that it would fail to offer the "whole of humanity back to the Father."

Aware of the potential for conflict over this and other subjects at the conference, Archbishop Runcie spoke about conflict in his opening address:

> Conflict can be destructive. It can also be creative. We are not here to avoid conflict, but to redeem it! At the heart of our faith is a cross, and not, as in some religions, an eternal calm.

Resolution 1 of the 1988 Lambeth Conference resolved "that each Province respect the decision and attitudes of other Provinces in the ordination or consecration of women to the episcopate, without such respect necessarily indicating acceptance of the principles involved, maintaining the highest possible degree of communion with the Provinces which differ." This resolution regularized the historic development of the priesthood of women of the churches in the Anglican Communion.

Furthermore, the resolution asked that the Archbishop of Canterbury appoint a commission to monitor and assist the churches of the Communion in continuing consultation with each other. He appointed the primate of the Church of Ireland, Archbishop Robert Eames, as chairman. This "Eames Commission" played an important role in maintaining communication as each province addressed the question of women in the priesthood and helped "ease" the transition among the provinces.

There were seventy-three resolutions at Lambeth 1988, reflecting the wide range of considerations confronting a global church.[1] A series of resolutions addressed ecumenical dialogues, including those with Lutherans, Orthodox churches, Reformed churches, the Roman Catholic Church (through the Anglican-Roman Catholic International Commission), Methodists, and the Baptist World Alliance. Other resolutions dealt with a wide range of social issues, including polygamy; Christ and culture; Palestine-

---

[1] The full report of the subjects and resolutions of the Lambeth Conference of 1988 can be found in the report entitled "The Truth Shall Make You Free," published for the ACC.

Israel relations; war, violence and justice; sexual abuse; conscientious objection, and various other issues.

One especially notable feature of the 1988 Lambeth Conference was the program arranged for the bishops' spouses, much of which was organized by Rosalind Runcie, the wife of the Archbishop of Canterbury. The spouses were welcomed at the Archbishop's palace in Canterbury and participated in many of the shared events on the campus of the University of Kent. After two full weeks, the conference ended with the Archbishop and Mrs. Runcie saying farewell to all of the participants as they left Canterbury Train Station. Soon after, I was pleased to receive a handwritten letter from Archbishop Runcie:

> Whichever way the Lambeth Conference is regarded
> by pundits, theologians, and critics, I regard it as a personal triumph for your commitment and organization
> ... and your flair for seeing possibilities.

Transition at Canterbury

Soon, it was time to organize a Primates' Meeting in Cyprus in 1989 and a meeting of the Anglican Consultative Council in Wales in 1990. In addition to these meetings, it was a time in which to concentrate on the development of the inter-Anglican networks through which the programs and ministries of the Communion could be coordinated.

One of the responsibilities of the Secretary General is to sit on the committee nominating a candidate for the office of Archbishop of Canterbury to the Prime Minister and the British monarch. With the retirement of Archbishop Runcie, it became my responsibility to join the committee nominating his successor. The Secretary General is a statutory member; other members of the committee were appointed by the General Synod of the Church of England and by the Diocese of Canterbury. The chairman was appointed by Prime Minister Margaret Thatcher. Our

*At a ceremony marking his retirement, Archbishop of
Canterbury Robert Runcie is seated in St. Augustine's chair,
center, and surrounded by the cathedral canons.
Van Culin is at far right.*

meetings were confidential, but I can report that the experience provided me with an inside look into the workings of the so-called "Establishment" of the Church of England. In preparation for my participation, I had asked all of the Anglican primates if they could suggest a candidate for me to put forward for nomination. The response was that the Primate of England should be nominated by the Church of England. This confirmed for me the fact that while the Archbishop of Canterbury has a global role as the central office of unity for the Communion—the *primus inter pares*, or 'first among equals'—there was no desire at the time to nominate a non-British candidate.

The committee's eventual nominee, the Rt. Rev.

Lady Eileen Carey and Archbishop George Carey.

George L. Carey, the Bishop of Bath and Wells, was approved by the Prime Minister and forwarded to the Queen for appointment. Soon after his enthronement in Canterbury Cathedral in 1991, I helped him prepare for his first meeting with Primates and members of the ACC. Later, Archbishop Carey wrote me a thoughtful note, saying, "I am so grateful to you for easing me into my new role so efficiently and so effectively nudging me along."

I served as Secretary General with Archbishop Carey for three interesting years. He presided at my last joint meeting with primates and the Anglican Consultative Council, held in February 1993 in Cape Town, South Africa, at the University of the Western Cape. The meeting was designed to deepen the relationship between two of the central bodies of the Anglican Communion. This was also a time of special historic, political, and social transitions in South Africa, following the release of Nelson Mandela from Robben Island. Archbishop Desmond Tutu arranged for Mandela to come and address our meeting. We realized that we were present at the "dawn" of a new South Africa, with the emergence of Mandela as a political and cultural leader. At the end of the meeting, I was presented with a South African painting in thanks for my years of service as Secretary General of the Anglican Communion. That painting hangs in my living room today.

A painting by the South African painter Stanley Hermans,
presented to Van Culin at the meeting of the Anglican
Consultative Council in 1993.

Ecumenical Involvements

During my years as Secretary General, I chaired the Committee of the Anglican Centre in Rome. The Centre was founded in 1966 following a meeting between Archbishop Ramsey and Pope Paul VI and is dedicated to developing relationships between the Anglican and Roman Catholic churches. It is located in the Palazzo Doria Pamphili, close to the Piazza Venezia. During these years, we were able to move the funding of the Centre from the Communion budget to an independent, self-governing organization. It continues to be a special Anglican presence in Rome, in touch with the Vatican.

Also during my time as Secretary General, I was a member of the Meeting of Secretaries of World Communions. The membership included representatives from the Vatican Secretariat for Unity and the Orthodox Ecumenical Patriarchate, as well as the Methodist, Lutheran, Baptist, and Reformed Secretariats and the World Council of

Van Culin with Pope John Paul II at the Vatican in Rome. The Most Rev. Joseph Abiodun Adetiloye, Anglican Archbishop of Nigeria, is at center.

Churches. We met to share information, and one of our most important efforts was to find a way to agree on a common date for Easter. Regrettably, we recognized that there were impediments within some of the traditions that made it difficult to agree at the time. I continue to believe that the effort to find a common date among the churches of the East and the West for the celebration of Christ's resurrection would inaugurate an historical development in our shared spiritual life.

On leaving office, I visited the Vatican Secretariat for Unity to say farewell. While Secretary General, I had at least two visits to their office every year as part of our ecumenical dialogues. During my farewell visit to the Secretariat, I discovered that they had arranged a private meeting for me with Pope John Paul II. I had first met the Pope previously over lunch in his private apartments with Archbishop Runcie, and I had been with the Pope on numerous visits to the Vatican. To be alone with him in his study, however, was memorable and inspiring. Notably, we discussed at one point the difference between "effects" and "affects" in ecclesiastical leadership. The Pope, who spoke excellent English, commented that while, in making decisions and seeking to lead, we may have an "effect," it remains the case that we can rarely achieve an "affect." In other words—even (and perhaps especially) in church circles—proclamation is one thing; acceptance is another.

The Pope's comment was germane to our ecumenical conversations—especially to the work of the Anglican-Roman Catholic International Commission, or ARCIC. Carefully chosen representatives meet to articulate in theological language the basis of our search for unity between the two churches. Over an extended period, an agreed statement is issued for study in the local churches. This is called the "reception process." The agreed statement is meant to "effect" relationships in the local churches. The responses of those churches vary considerably—the "affect" differs across local situations. The search for unity calls for more than an agreed-upon statement; it requires an *affectionate* response on the part of the local church. This highlights the challenge of helping local churches to accept growth to-ward unity.

Local Ties and Honors

During my twelve years in office as Secretary General, I was very fortunate to be a member of the parish of All Hallows by the Tower in the City of London, the oldest parish in the city, going back to Roman times. I had started my involvement there in the 1960s when the Rev. Philip "Tubby" Clayton was vicar and friend; he was the founder of Toc H, a ministry that began as a rest house in Belgium for troops fighting in the First World War and that grew into an international Christian service movement.

My association continued in the 1980s, when the Rev. Peter Delaney (who became Archdeacon of London) was vicar. My association with the parish provided me with a sense of church home, a center of worship and prayer, and a circle of supportive friends. At Peter Delaney's invitation, I became an active, participating member of the clerical staff, joining with them in celebrating the Eucharist and preaching. Later, I was honored to have Archbishop

Runcie dedicate a window in the church in my name. The window is the Compass Rose Window. The Archbishop dedicated it following the 1988 Lambeth Conference both to recognize my service as the Secretary General of the Anglican Communion (1983–95) and to mark the inauguration of ordination of women to the priesthood in the Communion.

The church of All Hallows had another "American connection" in that William Penn, founder of the state of Pennsylvania, was baptized there, and John Quincy Adams, fifth president of the United States, was married there.

During my time as Secretary General, I was installed as an Honorary Canon in a number of provinces in the Anglican Communion, including Nigeria, England, the United States, South Africa, and Jerusalem. In his letter appointing me a Provincial Honorary Canon in the Province of Southern Africa, Archbishop Desmond Tutu wrote,

> Sam, you are known and loved here in Southern Africa. This honor now expresses our love and appreciation of all that you continue to do for the Communion and this Province.

I hold honorary doctorates from Virginia Theological Seminary in Alexandria, Virginia, and General Theological Seminary in New York City. I was deeply moved and honored when, in her Honors List of 1995, the Queen appointed me an Honorary Officer of the British Empire, O.B.E. I was made a Freeman of the City of London by the

Lord Mayor of London, being the ninth non-British recipient of that honor.

Van Culin with Archbishop of Canterbury Robert Runcie and the vicar of All Hallow's by the Tower, The Ven. Peter Delaney, at the unveiling of a stained-glass window commemorating Van Culin's four decades of active priesthood, including his service as first Secretary General of the Anglican Communion.

THIS WINDOW IS GIVEN IN THANKSGIVING
FOR 35 YEARS OF PRIESTHOOD BY

CANON SAMUEL VAN CULIN

THE COMPASS ROSE IS THE SYMBOL OF THE
WORLD-WIDE ANGLICAN COMMUNION

DEDICATED BY
THE MOST REVD·& RT·HON·ROBERT RUNCIE
ARCHBISHOP OF CANTERBURY

ON ST·ANDREWS DAY
30TH NOVEMBER – 1990

Van Culin window at All Hallows by the Tower, London.
Courtesy Philip Chalk.

Retirement

In 1995, I retired as Secretary General and was succeeded by the Rev. John Peterson from the Province of Jerusalem and the Middle East, where he served as a missionary of the Episcopal Church. I moved to Canterbury, where I remain a Canon Emeritus at the cathedral. I had hoped for years that I could live in an "English cathedral town," and my nine retired years in Canterbury were the fulfillment of that dream. The Dean of the cathedral, the Very Rev. John Simpson, made me welcome and included me in much of its life. He arranged a cathedral apartment just at the edge of the cathedral grounds in the Burgate area, which I rented for the years that I lived there.

During those nine years, Dean Simpson and I often discussed his plans for the cathedral. Among them was the hope that he could expand facilities for education and hospitality. This required fundraising, and he hoped the Episcopal Church in the US would help. An opportunity to pursue this hope arose when the Rev. John Harper, the retired rector of St. John's, Lafayette Square in Washington, D.C., and his wife Barbie came to visit me in Canterbury. During dinner in my apartment with the Simpsons, the Dean asked John Harper if he would be willing to accept an invitation to lead an effort in the US to raise funds for expanding the educational and hospitality facilities at the cathedral. John accepted, and over the next few years, he organized a "Friends of Canterbury Cathedral US," or FOCCUS, which raised more than one million dollars for the Canterbury project. FOCCUS continues to support the Cathedral, and I am pleased to be a member of its Board of Trustees.

From my apartment windows, I watched the construction of the Lodge and education complex, which soon became the center of the cathedral's ministries of hospitality and education under the leadership of Simpson's successor, Dean Robert Willis. I was deeply inspired by the history, worship, and friendships that I experienced and continue to experience in Canterbury.

Van Culin at the National Cathedral in Washington, D.C.

Back in Washington

In 2004, I returned to Washington, D.C. My twenty-one years in London and Canterbury had been happy and productive, and I am grateful for the friendships and the unique experiences I was privileged to have there. But it was time to look ahead.

The opportunity came when the bishop of Washington, the Rt. Rev. John Chane invited me to settle at the Washington National Cathedral. The acting dean of the cathedral was the Rt. Rev. A. Theodore Eastman, retired bishop of Maryland and a longstanding close friend and associate. Ted and his colleagues welcomed me warmly, and Bishop Chane installed me as an honorary cathedral canon. Later, Dean Randolph Hollerith would make me canon for Anglican Communion Ministry. It is a title I am honored to carry.

I have found a spiritual home and many friends at the Washington National Cathedral. Over the years, I have

Three priests of the Episcopal Church, all from Hawaii and all Van Culins—Tom (left), Sam (center), and Drew—at class reunions at the Punahou School in Honolulu in 2013.

served as a celebrant and a preacher. In a way, my association with the National Cathedral completes a cycle in my ministry. The Cathedral has brought me back home to Washington, D.C., where I began my ministry at St. John's, Lafayette Square in June 1958. I understand that I now am the priest with the longest term of canonical residency in the Diocese of Washington, D.C. At my death, I will be buried in the Garth at the cathedral. I find that I no longer live a busy life, but I do live a full life.

A significant contribution to my full life now has been the rediscovery of my personal family. I had effectively been distant from my family since leaving Honolulu for Washington, and a period of more than forty years had passed. Since returning from England, I have enjoyed getting to know my brother's children—my niece Victoria (Tori) and her husband Randy and son Isaac, as well as her brother, my nephew Andrew (Drew). Drew and his wife Jessica chose to name their first child and son Sam, after me. This has added significantly to the "fullness" of my life, as there is now another Sam Van Culin growing up, along with his lovely sister, Catherine. My brother Tom was ordained an Episcopal priest in 1992, and his son, Drew, was ordained in 2000. Drew now serves as rector of Christ Church, Grosse Point, Michigan. There is something special about three Van Culins in the priesthood of the Episcopal Church at the same time. My brother died in November 2018. He had a long life of ministry, both as a layman and a priest, in the Episcopal Church. His funeral was at St. Andrew's Cathedral in Honolulu, where we were both baptized, confirmed, and ordained on different occasions, and where I served from 1955 to 1958. The liturgy at his funeral was celebrated in Hawaiian; some of his ashes were scattered in the Pacific Ocean off of Waikiki Beach and some were buried at Oahu's "Punchbowl," the National Memorial Cemetery of the Pacific.

As I watched my brother's children and grandchildren paddling a canoe off Waikiki, carrying his ashes, I was moved by a poignant realization: I was standing on the location at the Halekulani Hotel where I had stood as an eleven-year-old boy, looking out to sea and wondering, "What is beyond the horizon?" I realized also that my brother had gone where I would eventually follow— beyond the next and final human horizon.

I have managed to return to England almost every year for a month since returning to Washington. In addition to visiting friends and former associates in London and Canterbury in particular, I have attended the annual gathering in Oxford of the Guild for Pastoral Psychology. Meeting at Worchester College, the Guild, of which Carl Jung was founding patron, serves as "a meeting-place for those who wish to explore the religious and spiritual quest enhanced by the insights of psychology." Membership has included clergy, analysts, artists, counselors, and individuals whose lives have been enriched by the Jungian analytical experience.

I have engaged in Jungian analysis in New York City, London, and Zurich, and I have read much of the written work of Carl Jung over the years. That experience has helped me to understand my priestly vocation as responding to the invitation of Jesus to "take up your cross and follow me" (Matt 16:25). Jung spoke of the Cross as the symbol "for the integration of the opposites." The Cross is at the heart of the priestly vocation in the contemporary world.

I find a book recently written by Archbishop of Canterbury Justin Welby an important and helpful effort to explore the meaning of the Cross. In *The Power of Reconciliation,* the Archbishop says, "I write about peace and reconciliation in the sense of seeking relationships at all levels of human life that are resilient enough to have disagreements

Portrait of Van Culin courtesy of Danielle E. Thomas and the Washington National Cathedral.

without destruction." Peace is not found by avoiding conflict, he writes, but by "disagreeing well."

The book arises out of the recent years during which the Archbishop has sought to continue "gathering the Communion" in a world seeking new identities and moral affirmations. We live in an increasingly pluralistic society, and if the church is to continue proclaiming that we are called to love God and neighbor, we must be willing to examine the impediments to that message in our own lives. A very important initiative explained in this book is the

Archbishop's development of a "Difference Course" to help people reflect on many of their attitudes, convictions, and traditions that impede reconciliation.

I take it that what the Archbishop is describing is the need for an "examined life"—the need to reflect on the often unconscious motivations in our personal lives. In truth, this is the missional impulse in the Christian gospel.

As I reflect on the Cross and the "power of reconciliation," I think of my ordination at St. Andrew's Cathedral in Honolulu in 1955. During the service, we recited the Litany for Ordinations, saying, "We pray to you, Lord Christ, for the mission of the Church, that in faithful witness, it may preach the gospel to the ends of the earth." It has been my vocation as a priest, along with that of every man and woman who has taken the same vow, to help our church accomplish this mission. This vocation has filled my life with gratitude and joy.

There is a Cross at the heart of reconciliation, as the Anglican Communion and the wider world are discovering.

Afterword

THE RT. REV. ANTHONY POGGO

It is a privilege to write the afterword of this book on the life and ministry of the Reverend Canon Samuel Van Culin. Although I had heard many praiseworthy things about Canon Van Culin before becoming Secretary General, I only had the joy of meeting him in person when I visited Virginia Theological Seminary (VTS) in April 2023.

It is so encouraging to meet colleagues who know and understand one's own job and who can provide invaluable wisdom, wisdom that is also beautifully displayed in these pages.

Canon Van Culin's early life and ministry providentially prepared him for his worldwide ministry. God always ensures that the ministries and connections in earlier stages of our lives are not wasted: they are like building blocks for what God has in store for us later in life. Sam's involvement with the Overseas Mission Society and his role in the launch of a training initiative for Americans to work overseas through the Layman International was a training program for Sam. This led him to his role in the Church Center of the Episcopal Church. Sam's participation in three different General Conventions of the Episcopal Church (1955, 1958, and 1961) was again one of the ways God was training him for both his national and international roles.

I was not aware that Sam was involved in the Toronto Congress. I was interested to learn that the most famous of the outcomes of the congress, namely the Mutual Responsibility and Interdependence (MRI) initiative, was taken forward by the Episcopal Church in its 1964 Convention by the launch of the "Projects for Partnership" scheme. Again, this was part of God's plan in preparing Sam for his role when he was appointed in August 1976 as Executive for National and World Mission. This gave him the opportunity to connect U.S. dioceses with various overseas partners as well as other member churches in the Anglican Communion. Many of the contacts made were useful when Sam moved to London in 1983 to take on the role of Secretary General of the Anglican Consultative Council.

It was encouraging to read what the then Presiding Bishop, John Allin, wrote regarding Sam's appointment. He said that Sam was needed as Secretary General of the ACC and that although he would be missed by all in the Church Center in New York, he would now be serving the bigger Anglican Communion family. This reminded me of my own relocation from my role as Bishop of Kajo-Keji in 2016 to join Archbishop Justin Welby's Anglican

Communion team as his Adviser on Anglican Communion Affairs. This was not a popular move in Kajo-Keji. When some people complained to the then Primate of South Sudan, Archbishop Daniel Deng Bul, he told them that they should be glad that I was coming to serve the global Anglican Communion. This was positive for South Sudan because it would contribute to the larger Anglican Communion family.

Many of Sam's activities at the time remain central to the role of Secretary General. I was told to expect to visit all provinces of the Anglican Communion, to ensure that all voices are heard. Sam served as a pioneer in his own extensive travels across the Anglican Communion, modelling a best practice for his successors. To be sure, balancing these trips with the many other demands of the role is challenging. I have been grateful for the wisdom of Sam, and of others, in this regard.

Sam served on the committee appointed by the Anglican Communion to suggest ways to implement the recommendations of the MRI report from the 1963 Congress in Toronto. One of the key recommendations was to create a consultative body, which came to be known as the Anglican Consultative Council. This committee met in Kandy in Sri Lanka in June 1967. The committee wrote a draft constitution for the ACC which was submitted to the 1968 Lambeth Conference. All the provinces of the Anglican Communion had to approve the proposal for the creation of the ACC by at least a two thirds majority. The council held its first meeting in Limuru, Kenya in 1971. At the time of writing, we are now preparing for the nineteenth meeting of the ACC ("ACC-19"), which will be hosted by the Church of Ireland in 2026.

Sam's service as a member of the committee which met in Kandy, Sri Lanka, again gave him an inside view of what transpired in these discussions, which would have prepared him for his later work. He could not have known that he would later serve as Secretary General of the ACC in succession to Bishop John Howe, the first Executive Officer of the ACC from 1983.

When Sam was appointed as Secretary General, he received a warm welcome in London with a reception at Lambeth Palace hosted by then Archbishop of Canterbury, Robert Runcie, and his wife, Rosalind. Secretaries General need to work well with Archbishops of Canterbury and their staffs at Lambeth Palace. The Anglican Communion Office (ACO) exists to serve what we now call the four Instruments of Communion, namely, the Archbishop of Canterbury, the Lambeth Conference, the Primates' Meeting, and the Anglican Consultative Council. In the current structure, the Archbishop of Canterbury is the President of the ACC and convenes the Primates' Meeting as well as the Lambeth Conference. All the practical and logistical arrangements for these meetings are undertaken by the ACO as the Secretariat of the Communion, led by the Secretary General.

The ACO also ensures that resolutions and outcomes of

these meetings are implemented, by bringing them to the attention of provinces. Each province is autonomous and may choose to implement or ignore such outcomes. As the ACO is not the headquarters of the Anglican Communion, it does not have the powers of enforcement. Similarly, the Archbishop of Canterbury has no authority in any province beyond his own, save for a moral authority. Sam referred to what Archbishop Runcie said when he was asked to explain the role of the Archbishop of Canterbury. Archbishop Runcie said that "the job of the Archbishop of Canterbury is to gather the Communion, not to rule it." Today, we would say that the Archbishop plays that gathering role alongside the other primates, as a colleague among peers, and in concert with the ACO and ACC.

The Anglican Communion continues to work together through commissions and networks. Sam provides an important account of the idea for the networks in Singapore during the seventh meeting of the ACC in 1987. This included the inauguration of the office of the Anglican Communion Representative at the United Nations, which continues today.

One of Sam's first tasks when he took over as Secretary General was to organize a Primates' Meeting in Limuru, Kenya at the end of 1983. Among the things that the Archbishop of Canterbury wanted was to seek the advice of the primates on whether to hold another Lambeth Conference. The primates gave their nod for the convening of the 1988 Lambeth Conference. One of the phrases that caught my eye was Archbishop Runcie's statement that "I want each bishop to bring their diocese with them." This led to the convening of a series of regional meetings held around the Communion in Africa, Asia, the Americas, and the Middle East.

Archbishop Justin Welby began his archiepiscopacy by visiting all the primates in their own provinces to discuss the future of the Anglican Communion and the possibility of holding a Primates' Meeting and a Lambeth Conference. These visits were instrumental in enabling the next Primates' Meeting to take place in January 2016. One of the outcomes of this meeting was that the primates gave Archbishop Justin the go-ahead to plan for the next Lambeth Conference. As Archbishop Justin was keen that the agenda and plans for the Lambeth Conference should be consultative, he suggested Regional Primates' Meetings at which he, the CEO of the Lambeth Conference Company, and other senior staff might hear agenda items and concerns from the region. Another Primates' Meeting was convened in October 2017 in Canterbury, to update the primates and hear from them further thoughts and suggestions for the Lambeth Conference.

The importance of interpretation into different languages was one of the lessons that Sam learned when he spoke to Roman Catholic colleagues. Interpretation and translation enabled the success of the Bible studies at the 1988 Lambeth Conference. The organizers had to manage translation into Portuguese, Japanese, Swahili, Spanish, and English. Today, translation and interpretation remain more important than ever at all Anglican Communion meetings. As one family, no one should be linguistically disadvantaged. At the 2022 Lambeth Conference, interpretation was provided in the foregoing languages as well as in French, Korean, Burmese, and Juba Arabic.

At the 1988 Lambeth Conference, disagreement about the ordination of women to the priesthood and episcopate played a prominent role. This question remains a bone of contention in some provinces. Divisions about human sexuality and Anglican identity have dominated all meetings of the Communion since Lambeth Conference 1998. Resolution I:10 of that conference has remained omnipresent, above all in its claim that "[we] cannot advise the legitimising or blessing of same sex unions nor ordaining those involved in same gender unions." Looking ahead, reconciliation may be possible insofar as the Communion can learn to accommodate sustained disagreements, without seeking to erase them prematurely. We are learning slowly to treat one another with respect, to persevere patiently in hard conversations, and not to give up on truth and agreement, even and especially when they are hard won.

Archbishops Runcie and Welby have approached conflict resolution similarly. Sam cited Archbishop Runcie's conviction that "conflict can be destructive. It can also be creative. We are not here to avoid conflict, but to redeem it!" Archbishop Justin has spoken of "disagreeing well."

This is a message that the Anglican Communion needs more than ever if it is to maintain and deepen its unity.

Sam describes the role he played in the process for appointing the next Archbishop of Canterbury. The Secretary General sits, as a non-voting member, on the nominating committee. A recent decision of the General Synod of the Church of England has stipulated that five additional members drawn from the five regions of the Communion will also serve on the Crown Nominations Commission for the See of Canterbury. The Secretary General will remain a non-voting member.

As Secretary General, Sam also chaired the Committee of the Anglican Centre in Rome (ACR). Today, a board of governors oversees the work of the ACR and supports its Director. The Secretary General serves on this board. The ACO's Director of Unity, Faith and Order serves as Secretary.

Sam attended meetings of Secretaries of World Communions. These still take place on an annual basis and are enormously valuable. No detailed minutes are taken, beyond agreed action points. We update each other on our latest affairs, questions, and challenges. The meeting comprehends representatives from the Vatican, the Orthodox Ecumenical Patriarchate, the Methodist, Lutheran, Baptist, and Reformed Secretariats, the World Council of Churches, and several others. Sam mentions that a common date for Easter was mooted during his time. This question is being asked again, but remains difficult to resolve.

Sam's continued support for Canterbury Cathedral through the Friends of Canterbury Cathedral U.S. is a blessing. One of Sam's successors, the Reverend John Peterson, similarly plays a pivotal role with the Compass Rose Society. He and others are taking the lead to develop an Endowment Fund, to protect and advance the life and work of the Anglican Communion Office.

I am truly grateful to Sam for the opportunity to reflect here on the enormous fruitfulness of his life and ministry. The many continuities across the decades are both comforting and marvelous to consider. Amid many challenges and complexities, our dear global family has continued to grow and mature, thanks to the careful planting and watering of our forebears. Of course, God gives the growth (1 Cor 3:6).

I hope that readers of this book will continue to pray for Sam, and also for me and my colleagues in the secretariat of the Anglican Communion, as we seek to answer the call of God, to love and serve our family of churches. *To God be the glory, great things he has done*—and continues to do.

The Rt. Rev. Anthony Poggo
Secretary General of the Anglican Communion

Contributor Biographies

The Right Reverend Anthony Poggo is the current Secretary General of the Anglican Communion. In this role, he leads the staff team at the Anglican Communion Office, the international secretariat serving the four "Instruments of Communion"—sometimes called the "Instruments of Unity." These are the Archbishop of Canterbury, the Primates' Meeting, the Anglican Consultative Council, and the Lambeth Conference.

Born in 1964, in what is now South Sudan, Bishop Anthony and his siblings were taken by his father—an Anglican priest—and his mother into Uganda to flee the first Sudanese Civil War. In 1973, at the age of nine, he returned with his family to South Sudan. After graduating from Juba University with a degree in Management and Public Administration, he joined the ecumenical mission agency Scripture Union. While there, he felt a need for theological training and gained an MA in Biblical Studies from the Nairobi International School of Theology in Kenya. He then returned to Uganda to minister to Sudanese refugees with Scripture Union. The Bishop of Kajo-Keji, the Right Rev Manasseh Binyi Dawidi—who himself was serving the Sudanese refugees in exile in Uganda—asked him to consider ordination.

He was ordained a Deacon in 1995 and a Priest in 1996 and continued working for Scripture Union before joining Across, a Christian mission agency working in Sudan from Nairobi, leading the charity's publishing arm. While there he studied for an MBA in publishing at Oxford Brookes University in England. He rose through the ranks at Across, eventually becoming the Executive Director of the organization.

In 2007 he was elected Bishop of Kajo-Keji, a position he held until 2016 when he moved to Lambeth Palace to support the Archbishop of Canterbury, Justin Welby, as his Adviser on Anglican Communion Affairs. On September 1, 2022, Bishop Anthony became the Secretary General of the Anglican Communion, the eighth person to hold the post. The role has its origins at the Lambeth Conference of 1958, after which the post of Executive Officer of the Communion was created. The job title changed to its current one after the creation of the Anglican Consultative Council in 1968.

The Rev. A. Katherine Grieb serves as the Director of the Center for Anglican Communion Studies and as an affiliated faculty member at Virginia Theological Seminary. She joined the VTS faculty in 1994. Her expertise includes Greek language, New Testament Interpretation, Romans, Hebrews, social justice, Biblical storytelling, and theatre. Before coming to VTS, she taught at Bangor Theological Seminary. She published *The Story of Romans* in 2002 with Westminster John Knox. She co-edited *The Word Leaps the Gap*, published with Eerdmans in 2008. She is currently writing a book on Scriptural Reasoning.

Dr. Grieb received her B.A. in Philosophy and Religion from Hollins University, her J.D. from Columbus School of Law (Catholic University of America), her M.Div from VTS, her Ph.D. (with distinction) in Religious Studies (Theology) from Yale University, and her L.L.M. (with distinction) in Canon Law from Cardiff University School of Law.

Ordained to the diaconate and priesthood in the Diocese of Washington in 1983, she has served part-time at St. Stephen & the Incarnation Episcopal Church in Washington, DC for almost thirty years.

Dr. Grieb was a member of the Theology Committee of the House of Bishops of the Episcopal Church and represented the Episcopal Church at the World Council of Churches Plenary Session in 2009. She was one of seven theologians asked to write *To Set Our Hope on Christ*, in response to the Windsor Report. She was a member of the Anglican Communion Covenant Design Group.

Dr. Grieb was also a member of IASCUFO (the Inter-Anglican Standing Commission on Unity Faith and Order) of the Anglican Communion and has taught for many years at the Canterbury Scholars program at Canterbury Cathedral. A popular preacher and teacher, she leads ordination retreats and theological Bible studies for diocesan clergy days and other church groups.

Made in the USA
Columbia, SC
23 June 2025